Sing to me

Mani Rao

Sing to me

of Greek myths

IPSI CHAPBOOK 2.3

University of Canberra
International Poetry Studies Institute
Series editor: Paul Munden

RECENT
WORK
PRESS

UNIVERSITY OF CANBERRA

International Poetry Studies Institute
Faculty of Arts and Design
University of Canberra
Canberra, Australia
http://ipsi.org.au

Poems © Mani Rao 2019
Design: Caren Florance

ISBN 978-0-6485537-7-9

CONTENTS

Sing To Me	1
Peace Treaty	4
Father's Day	5
My Daughter Philomela	7
Cadmus is History	9
Jove's Collar	10
As Promised Tithonus	11
Postcard Aphrodite	13
Fêted	18
Ding Dong Bell	24
Iliad Blues	25
In The Shower Thinking of Actaeon	26
Aphrodite:	27
On The Tail	28
Venus and Adonis	29
Or Us	30
Simile	31
Cupid and Psyche	32
Midas a Casino in Vegas	33
Poem, Sisyphus	34
Biography & books	*37*

SING TO ME

O' muses excuse
this non-descript call I

Wonder who
among you apt who
interested

Greek and Sanskrit
A must

I mean not words
Spaces

where two species
      gods/humans
intersect

O'

Calliope	Erato	Thalia
Clio	Melpomena	Urania
Euterpe	Polyhymnia	Terpsichore

Magic nine
all-girl cast

Dad voluptuary
Stepmother hung by the heels

Constant news of half-sisters
Mother in deep glue

When family's this dys
Your friends are poets

Mt Parnassus at your
Apollo-dance

Sappho plays on
Trade for a tradition

Homer restless
Ovid morbid

Blake who met Ezekiel
Dante Virgil

Come one two three nine
Take turns if you tire

You're Kali for Kalidasa
Ganesha for Vyasa

For Lorca duende for Merril
a red-winged bat

Welcome the furies
Alecto   Magaera   Tisiphone

Justices of peace
We'll need them too

Around orchards Grecian
On battlefields Trojan

In Shiva's realm inside
Hanuman's heart

Gods are us

Dear reader, I trust you have met the cast of this poem already, or – with the internet so ubiquitous, please get acquainted on your own. If I do the introductions for some of the other poems, it won't be because you are a stranger, or lack the skill.

PEACE TREATY

What if Helen died

Cuckold crows
Husband recalls
Body, face, rites

Once broad Trojan devils now
cower in the shadows of walls
Fearing skywitnesses
Quaking at birdshit

Our boy came back
from overseas with a
souvenir egg that ticked

A runaway wife's a rotten prize
Unwanted alive
And dead

FATHER'S DAY

Stop wheels
Hector's hurting
Priam cries
Dusty from playing in the yard, Hector

Astyanax wails
Faint Andromache
Hecuba lactates

On Hecuba's weeping breasts
Rest Priam's drooping cheeks

Whose guts garland
the dogs of Troy
Not Patroclus'

Intact elevated
Body fêted
A high friendship keeps you
in good stead

Your funeral games over now
Release, Achilles, release Hector

A man who grieves for a boy
must have a soft spot
A man Hephaestus shields
must be made of flesh

His heels I'll cuff with my wrists
His knuckles I'll press my lips

Three children walked in hand in hand
Paris, Helen, and Troy's ghost
waiting to bloat
Priam's been waiting since

Cast:
Achilles: death
Hector: dead
Patroclus: young dead friend of Achilles
Priam: father
Hecuba: mother
Andromache: wife
Astyanax: son
Paris: brother
Hephaestus: ironsmith, god,
*   builder of Achilles' shield*

MY DAUGHTER PHILOMELA

The desire at the back of it all the
Right of a maker

      Your
Instinct draws love
Trust commands duty

Little Philomela
You knead my face-putty playdough-nose
You enter verbs prod nouns
Body, a fact you do not separate yet

Isn't it fun   running in the open   conquest of
trees   wrists   knees crunchy hair

Twirling in a new dress   Five husbands gawk
while Draupadi shuddering   lockjawed   what's
thoughts   where's mind   whose funpark   how to be
wrapped   Krishna

Arms crossed   knees fetal   your sleeping position's Leda

Every age imposes its season on you
You regardless permissive

O Philomela, a dog's fooled when lover returns as thief
Jatayu's goosed at Sita's heist
I did not even search his face
I thought him son his
Ardor manner procedure
Honored your sister

Now nightingales
Pity Tereus's father

Parent, place the snakes on Medusa's head

Who's why: Philomela, raped by her brother-in-law, Tereus, and then locked up. Tereus cuts off her tongue to ensure her silence. Philomela reveals the gory details to her sister Procne by weaving the story into a tapestry. Procne and Philomela kill Itys, Tereus and Procne's son, and serve him up to Tereus at dinner. Finally, Philomela turns into a nightingale to sing her story forever. | Draupadi – in the Mahabharata, stripped by the Kaurava brothers in public, prays to Krishna for help | Sita – in the Indian epic, Ramayana, abducted by Ravana | Jatayu – vulture who confronts Ravana's airplane with Sita on board; he loses, but proves an informant to Rama about the direction of Ravana's flight. | Leda – raped by a swan who is really Zeus.

CADMUS IS HISTORY

Stacked with crawl
The dermis malignant
These jungle skins are one
As Cadmus walks they sync

Don't come back without her begins his story
Exile begins a hero

Above the ground the trees appear various
He looks at the pointed faces leaves held like shields
His immediate hand darts to hilt

What falls is trunk
Any arborist will tell you that
You can't uproot history
History's staunch
Axes scratch graffiti

For details go to Ovid
I just give
the gist of it we
confront what we are we
become what we battle

History: Europa has been abducted by Jove. Brother Cadmus goes on a rescue mission. When he vanquishes a pesky dragon and sows its teeth in the ground, warriors spring up from these teeth, and the battle intensifies. After much back and forth, he (thinks he) wins. Not so fast, says the dragon's master, Ares, who demands compensation. Cadmus has to serve Ares for eight years. Later, after a long, heroic life, Cadmus metamorphoses into a snake.

JOVE'S COLLAR

How nice to have a wife
Who's also sister
You fornicate in the street
Then go home to eat

Those who like to bring up Europa, Io, Semele, Ganymede, Callisto and Leto are just jealous. Jove, smart enough to marry sister Juno, and smart enough to be chief of gods.

AS PROMISED TITHONUS

There'll be clusters ... presses ... drinks ...
Aurora runs
Aurora reddens

In the vineyard
by the corky
tendrils on the
stalks:
    Raisins

Aurora (goddess, dawn) asks Jupiter to grant her beloved mortal Tithonus immortality, but forgets to ask for youth. Typical.

POSTCARD APHRODITE

   1.

Ouranos leaned and pinched her nipples
Gaia forgot her sons lay in ambush
Even before he detached his thighs flanking the mountains her limbs
   arched for the meeting
Half swooning for his eyes leisurely grazing
It was not a memory   had never occurred
He was always so testy   (sons can be so crazy)
Recurrent dreams of a blade slicing his neck his blood seeding
   her body
When they sliced his testicles instead
His hands full on her breasts
Jerked a seizure
She ejaculated disbelief
Ouranos drained
Gaia sank

2.

Bright downward slash above
ruddy ocean below what
remains of sky

His pouches open paratroopers

Be anxious it's messy out there
Wind reluctant
Waves nervous

Then laugh O'how indifferent wave
of average height & no distinction
lands the prize

3.

Recall that other time when the leaky punk Raktabija 'bloodseed'
battled Kali
The more she hacked
the more he sprouted

Then Tongue stretched
between Earth and Sky

Licked each drop
as it fell

4.

Fresh froth breaks
Bubbles on speed
Champagne-solemn

Water animates
Hands breasts waist
Crimped hair
Signature

Exactly when does she express her face
Translucent sea-squiggle
Aphrodite

Okeanos marks the moment with a pause

Every wave rises
Reflects
Aphrodite gallery

5.

What is Aphrodite made of?

The impossible desire
Carried by rivers
Buried in ocean

You and I know it is memory
Gaia's
Aphrodite has none

Of one parent
Unconflicted
She heads for America

6.

One hundred and fifty feet stature
Shipwrecked hero
Face of commander

Beached on Ellis
Plankton-stained
Gulliver comes to mind

Little people probe her
Robe her
Hand her a torch
Hoist her on a pedestal
Crown her Statue Liberty

Poised since then
Open oyster shell

Desire ... Liberty

FÊTED

1.

What does Odysseus do when
the Odyssey is done

Memory's man
House on fire
The story ate it all

Back from Iraq
Busy being a shape
A guard

Sleeps in the old bed
Dines the old way
Visitors none

The front hall scrubbed clean
All of Ithaca's young men
chatting in Hades

It's all about the oil they say
Finite fire

Odysseus, son of Laertes, father of Telemachus,
husband of constant Penelope, family man

A long night
One half in a dream the other half
awake thinking about it

Over and over again of Helen
to the countrywomen

To the one-eyed scarecrow
in the fields said Nobody

2.

Another war-veteran Prometheus

Dented de-fizzed
Rocket to space-junk fell

Wayward washing
Ragged upon the crags

Flooded by the moon a startled thief

From the day he is engorged and cannot hide
till the day he is mute and will not show

In the shadow of the eagle he sees keeping watch

A luscious rested tongue
and thirsts for it

3.

Bheeshma chooses when to die
after farewells, speeches and a drink

Last man standing Yudhistira
has a friend a dog

The rest are soldiers, trees
Armour
Leaves
Star tips

End of day survivors
count spaces at the table

Face down at the bottom of that trench
Lots of hands and legs

4.

A child-minotaur branded monster
Thrown in a maze

Expect a labyrinth
A story

Alone uncastrated public object Minotaur
awaits a hero

We want a dizzying battle
Dodge! light-footed Theseus

Minotaur froths
Prisoner on D-day

5.

Arjuna retorts:

What do you know, Krishna,
what it is to be human?

Infant, on your knees
Excruciating waiting on teeth

From alphabet-soup
to the world
Pregnant, determinate uterus
Milk in your breasts
Sleeping Dreaming
Two hands two legs
Breath, bowels
Decrepit in the mirror
What do you know, Krishna

DING DONG BELL

The jetty's out
Who's at bay
War-mongrels Hera Athena

Stout Menelaus
Slender Paris
Homer leads the charge

Imperfection haunts beauty
So imagination can rule
Helen haunts imagination

In the centre of her forehead
Bloodthirsty star of the sea

What a naughty boy was that to try to drown poor pussy cat.

ILIAD BLUES

I like battles out at sea
Hot spur
Cold water
Blood swimming both ways
Salty meetings
Sharks due
At the end
Level blue

IN THE SHOWER THINKING OF ACTAEON

Gaily the nymphs pretend
to man her prudity
Hard after a hunt Diana
flirts water at Actaeon

STILL IN THE SHOWER THINKING OF ACTAEON

What Ovid does not offer
What Slavitt does not explain
It was the water I say
It was the water she
Squirted when you gawked
that masked your trail

Your curs fell on you
Deaf to Actaeon

Chaste Diana, hunting, bathing, surrounded by nymphs ... a gay life! Along comes a man, Actaeon, who stumbles upon the nudes and is duly cursed. Actaeon beats a retreat, goes back into the jungle and is mauled by his hunting dogs. Does mere looking have such consequences? You'd think a liberal translator like David Slavitt might have a theory.

APHRODITE:

Amorous
but no amour?

Your cock-tip smiles
spurting
moonbeam

There's a mouth
Doesn't lie

ON THE TAIL

What did you
do

with the bees
Hermes

Every which way
according to
the ithyphallic cacti

Ingenious Hermes steals Apollo's cows and lays confusing tracks to avoid detection. Apollo catches him by bribing a shepherd who was witness to the deed. Hermes was considered a phallic god of boundaries, so his name was engraved on wayside marker stones.

VENUS AND ADONIS

Exactly the
accent I like
Olive in mouth

Let's
    in the orchard
        pips around us

Promise me you'll
Speak
Greek

What are you waiting for?
The moon won't get any fuller nor
Venus more voluptuous

Adonis prefers to hunt   not
be chased   in any case
Mama Love's
too Romanesque for his taste

Venus is sticky and won't let Adonis go. What makes Greek heroes addictive? Why are Roman goddesses insufferable? Hidden in the resistance Adonis feels, the strong calling of death.

OR US

Whose story isn't Orpheus

You've been in Hell made a mistake been afraid you've got song
    you're prophecy you're God and you're not
Appreciated decapitated
At the height of a party your wife keels over
That you don't want her back you're guilty in fidelity you turn gay
    the Maenads have a field day   Maenads are our mothers

Orpheus starts a band
'The Regrets'

Dark dark dark dark
Tar tar us
Place as place
Grey gag
Absent air

SIMILE

Narcissus drowning in onlyness
The rest in duplicity

Ovid does not recommend being single. He punishes Narcissus for spurning Echo. I prefer to go with Tiresias, who said Narcissus would live to be old if he did not know himself first. Self-knowledge is a young flower with a bad reputation.

CUPID AND PSYCHE

To p on you
To quote myself

MIDAS A CASINO IN VEGAS

Talk to me, goldfish
Where's Titanic?

Fancy a gold apple
It's greed only if you're hungry

Lady Luck just wants a fuck
You don't need no PhD in Alchemy

POEM, SISYPHUS

Moon, Sisyphus
Full
Null

Life, Sisyphus
Chain

Who knows how many

Days in the life
of Brahma

Pebble, Sisyphus
On a beach
    Wave
    Wave
    Wave
Polishing

Up there slick
stars who made it

You know how Sisyphus had to roll a massive rock up a steep hill, and how it would roll back down again. But, do you know, a day in the life of Brahma = 4.32 billion years. So is a night. Brahma's life of a hundred years (36,000 days) = 311.04 trillion human years. Human life is not manifest during Brahma's night.

Mani Rao is the author of nine books of poetry, two books in translation from Sanskrit and an anthropological study of mantra practice. Mani's essays and poems have appeared in such journals as *Poetry magazine, Omniverse, Fulcrum, Interim, Iowa Review, Meanjin, Tinfish, Wasafiri, Washington Review, West Coast Line,* and *Zoland Poetry,* and in anthologies – W.W. Norton's *Language for a New Century,* Penguin's *60 Indian Poets,* and the *Bloodaxe Book of Contemporary Indian Poets.* She was a writing resident at Omi Ledig House (2018), the Iowa International Writing Program (2005 and 2009) and the 2006 University of Iowa International Programs.

BOOKS BY MANI RAO

Living Mantra: Mantra, Deity and Visionary Experience Today
    (Palgrave Macmillan Contemporary Anthropology of Religion, 2019)
New & Selected Poems (Poetrywala, 2014)
Kalidasa For the 21st Century Reader (Aleph Books, 2014))
Bhagavad Gita (Autumn Hill Books, 2010; Fingerprint Press, 2015)
Ghostmasters (Chameleon Press, 2010)
100 Poems: Selected Poems 1985-2005 (Chameleon Press, 2005)
Echolocation (Chameleon Press, 2003; Math Paper Press, 2014)
Salt (Asia 2000 Ltd, 2000)
The Last Beach (Asia 2000 Ltd, 1999)
Living Shadows (HKADC, 1997)
Catapult Season (Writers Workshop Calcutta, 1993)
Wingspan (Writers Workshop Calcutta, 1987)

www.manirao.com

IPSI: INTERNATIONAL POETRY STUDIES INSTITUTE

The International Poetry Studies Institute (IPSI) is part of the Centre for Creative and Cultural Research, Faculty of Arts and Design, University of Canberra. IPSI conducts research related to poetry, and publishes and promulgates the outcomes of this research internationally. The institute also publishes poetry and interviews with poets, as well as related material, from around the world. Publication of such material takes place in IPSI's online journal Axon: Creative Explorations (www.axonjournal.com.au). IPSI's goals include working – collaboratively, where possible – for the appreciation and understanding of poetry, poetic language and the cultural and social significance of poetry. The institute also organises symposia, seminars, readings and other poetry-related activities and events.

IPSI CHAPBOOK SERIES

The IPSI Chapbook Series publishes new work by leading poets from Australia and beyond. The chapbooks feature extended selections beyond the scope of most journals, highlighting innovative work by poets both new and established. The series is linked to an international program of poets in residence at the University of Canberra.
Series Editor: Paul Munden.

CCCR: CENTRE FOR CREATIVE & CULTURAL RESEARCH

The Centre for Creative and Cultural Research (CCCR) is IPSI's umbrella organisation and brings together staff, adjuncts, research students and visiting fellows who work on key challenges within the cultural sector and creative field. A central feature of its research concerns the effects of digitisation and globalisation on cultural producers, whether individuals, communities or organisations.

www.ingramcontent.com/pod-product-compliance
Ingram Content Group UK Ltd.
Pitfield, Milton Keynes, MK11 3LW, UK
UKHW021323180426
11947UKWH00017B/1409